The Deeside Line
W Stewart Wilson

The original station of Aberdeen was built in 1867 by John Morgan. In his long and varied career he was responsible for a number of notable buildings, including the frontage to Marischal College, the Central Library and the Northern Insurance Building (known locally as the Monkey House). He was also involved in planning Rosemount Viaduct. In 1887 he built for himself the Gothic style house on Queens Road known as Rubislaw House. The Joint Station consisted of a main booking office in the centre, with the booking offices for the Caledonian Railway and the Great North of Scotland Railway on either side. An early criticism was that the station acted as a form of wind tunnel, making it draughty for passengers which to some extent had been improved with the screen which had been added to just above the carriage roof level. This view is of the original station in its latter days with on the left, a Caledonian express about to leave for the south, and on the right the Great North's Deeside Express for Ballater.

The exterior of this famous station at Ballater was destroyed by fire in May 2015 but hopefully will be restored in the near future to form an information centre, library and restaurant as well as recreating the former Royal waiting room and housing the replica Royal carriage which was relatively undamaged. On the square outside the station, marking the boundary of railway property, are five diamond shaped flagstones inscribed GNSR as a reminder of former days.

© W Stewart Wilson, 2016
First published in the United Kingdom, 2016,
by Stenlake Publishing Ltd.
www.stenlake.co.uk
ISBN 9781840337631

The publishers regret that they cannot supply copies of any pictures featured in this book.

Printed by
P2D Books, 1 Newlands Rd,
Westoning, Bedford, MK45 5LD

Acknowledgements

I should like to thank all those who have given of their local knowledge including Gordon Casely, Jim Henderson, David Jamieson, Keith Jones, Michael Robson and The Royal Deeside Preservation Society.

Further Reading

Many books have been written about the Deeside Railway. The author found the following of particular interest and recommends them to those who wish to explore the Old Deeside Line in more detail. They are listed in chronological order of the original publication date. Those interested in finding out more are advised to contact their local bookshop, reference library or the Great North of Scotland Railway Association. Detailed information on the Deeside Way can be found on its website.

The Great North of Scotland Railway by Sir M Barclay-Harvey, Locomotive Publishing Co., 1940
The Royal Deeside Line by A D Farr, David and Charles, 1968
Stories of Royal Deeside's Railway by A D Farr, Kestrel Books, 1971
The Deeside Line by Dick Jackson, Great North of Scotland Railway Association, 1994
Royal Deeside's Railway by Dick Jackson, Great North of Scotland Railway Association, 1999
The Railways of Aberdeen by Keith Jones, Great North of Scotland Railway Association, 2000
Aberdeenshire's Lost Railways by Gordon Stansfield, Stenlake Publishing, 2000

Introduction

Before the Railway

The turnpike road replacing the old Deeside road was completed in three sections; in 1798 from Aberdeen as far as Mills of Drum, by 1802 it had reached Charleston of Aboyne but it was not until 1855 that the new road reached Braemar. Transport on Deeside was by coach and in the *New Deeside Guide* by James Brown (Joseph Robertson) published in 1843, we get an idea of the time taken for the journey. 'The Mail Coach leaves Aberdeen every morning at seven o'clock – and letters must be put into the Post Office by twenty minutes past six. It reaches Banchory at half-past nine – Kincardine O'Neil at eleven – Charleston of Aboyne about half-past eleven, and Ballater at one'.

The Line to Banchory

It was in 1845 that a board was formed to consider the building of a Deeside railway and so improve communications and travel. It was estimated that the cost of building a single line along the north bank of the Dee to Banchory would cost £95,000, or £220,000 to reach Aboyne. An Act for building of a railway from Ferryhill to Charleston of Aboyne received Royal Assent on 5th July 1846 but there were to be delays until the Great North of Scotland Railway had completed its temporary station at Ferryhill in early 1850. Negotiations then began with landowners for the building of the first section of the line and on 28th May 1852 the Deeside Railway Company obtained Royal Assent for a railway from Aberdeen and terminating at or near the Free Church at Banchory. At that time the Free Church in Banchory was on the north side of the Aberdeen to Aboyne turnpike immediately west of what is now Raemoir Road. Less than six weeks later, on 5th July 1852, Mrs. Kinloch of Park House, the wife of Alexander Kinloch, one of the directors of the Deeside Railway, cut the first turf near the Mains of Drum.

The laying of the new line went ahead and the new railway was ready for its first passengers on 7th September 1853. Two hundred invitations were issued for the official opening of the line at Ferryhill Station, Aberdeen. The following day the service opened for the public with stations at Cults,

Banchory village in the mid 19th century soon after the Deeside Line was opened ending the need for the mail coach

Murtle, Culter, Park, Mills of Drum, Crathes Castle and Banchory. Initially there were three trains a day, taking about an hour to travel the 16¾ miles. Stations at Milltimber and Drum were provided in the following year and soon after a station was opened at Ruthrieston. In 1863 the private platform at Crathes Castle and the small station at Mills of Drum were closed and replaced by a new station at Crathes on the site of the old platform. Ease of transport to Aberdeen by railway was also desired by those living south of the river, and bridges were built to allow access to stations where previously ferries and fords had been the only means of crossing the Dee. The popularity of Deeside was further enhanced by Queen Victoria who paid her first visit to the old Balmoral Castle in 1848. She so enjoyed it that in 1852 the estate was bought and a new castle was built, completed in 1855. The Deeside Railway was instantly popular with the Royal family and on Thursday 13th October 1853, just a month after the opening of the line, the Queen and Prince Albert made the journey from Banchory to Ferryhill. The Lord Provost and the other dignitaries met the Royal party to bid them farewell to Deeside and to promise them a warm welcome again. Guild Street Station in Aberdeen was opened in August 1854 and Ferryhill Junction was then closed for passenger traffic.

With the opening of the line to Banchory the Deeside coach to Banchory was no longer required. Alex Inkson McConnachie in his book *Deeside* published in 1893 remarks – 'before the construction of the Deeside Railway the beauties of the valley were little known, and at the opening few believed the line would prove remunerative'.

Banchory to Aboyne

Prosperous the line was, and in November 1856 plans were announced to extend the line from Banchory to Aboyne for which Royal Assent was granted on 27th July 1857. The first turf was cut on 2nd October near Charleston of Aboyne by the Marchioness of Huntly. Unlike the proposed plan of 1846, this time the route was not to pass through Kincardine O'Neil but to leave Banchory and head in a more northerly direction to Lumphanan before returning south to Aboyne. The first passenger train ran on the extended line to Aboyne on 2nd December 1859 with intermediate stations at Glassel, Torphins, Lumphanan and Dess.

Aboyne to Ballater

It was now inevitable that there would be a proposal for a further extension of the line to reach the whole of Deeside. Initially the plan had been to extend the line to Braemar but this was amended and the terminal was set to be Ballater with a further one and half miles to Bridge of Gairn to be used for goods traffic only, but this section of track was never laid. The route to Braemar would have passed close to Balmoral Castle and this was abandoned in May 1865 when Queen Victoria objected 'wishing the upper part of the Dee Valley to be preserved as a natural Highland region'. Royal Assent for the Aboyne to Ballater railway was given on 5th July 1865 and the ceremony of cutting the first turf was held on 7th September 1865 by Mrs. Farquharson of Invercauld. Less than thirteen months later on 17th October 1866 the first train reached Ballater with an intermediate station at Dinnet. An additional station at Cambus O' May was opened in 1876.

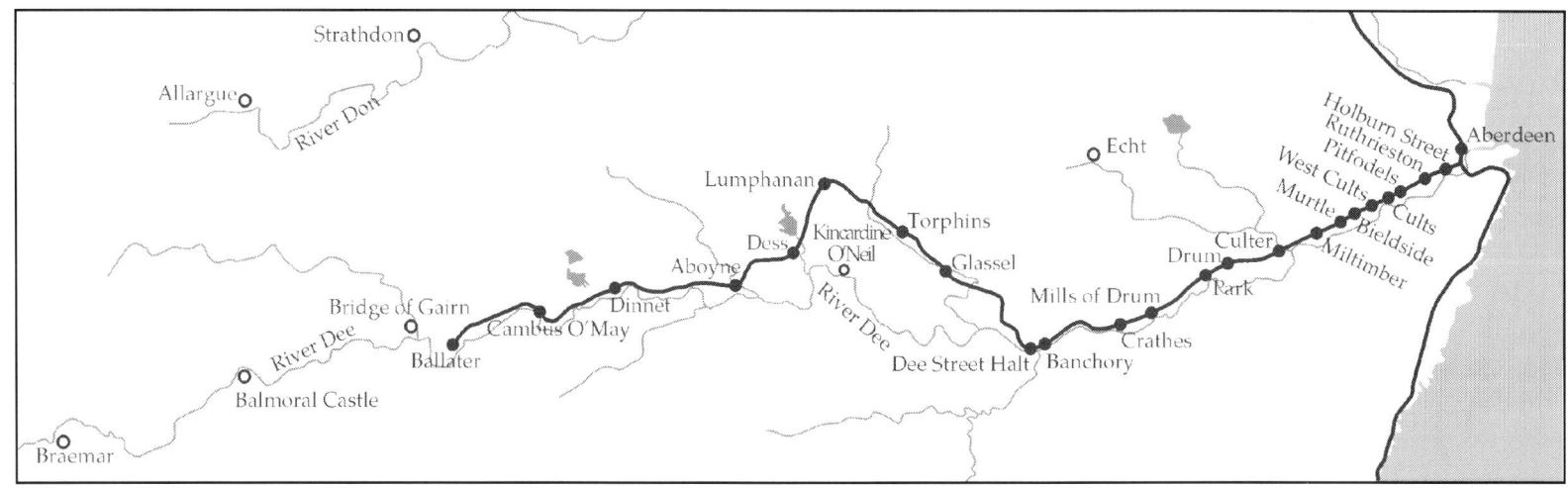

Changes of Ownership

In 1876 the Deeside Railway Company was absorbed by the Great North of Scotland Railway (GNSR). In 1923 it became the London and North Eastern Railway (LNER) before being absorbed by British Railways in 1948.

The Suburban Service to Culter

Lower Deeside became a favourite place for the wealthy merchants and businessmen of the city to build some beautiful houses, many of which survive to this day. As a result there was a need to provide reliable transport to the city and the railway track between Aberdeen and Culter was doubled thus enabling a regular suburban train service (known as the *Subbies*) to be introduced in 1894. New stations were opened at Holburn Street, Pitfodels, and West Cults with a station at Bieldside being added in 1897. The journey, stopping at seven intermediate stations along the route, took a mere 21 minutes. By the end of the 19th century the Joint Station was proving inadequate for the increased rail usage and in 1909 a Suburban Booking office was built on the corner of Bridge Street and Guild Street. The location was connected to Platform 9 which was used for the service to Culter. In 1928 a Sunday service was introduced for the first time but in 1937 because of the competing bus service the suburban train service ceased operations and the stations opened in 1894 along with those at Ruthrieston, Bieldside, Murtle and Milltimber were closed. The Beeching Report, published in 1963, was a death sentence to the Deeside line and despite many local petitions, the passenger train from Ballater to Aberdeen ran on Saturday 26th February 1966.

The Deeside Way

The tracks were removed, and the former line is now a popular path known as The Deeside Way and is used by walkers and cyclists with many sections also suitable for horses. The route follows the line of the Old Royal Deeside Railway from Aberdeen, starting at Duthie Park and as far as Banchory. It then passes through woodland and farmland by way of Scolty and Potarch to Kincardine O'Neil before rejoining the old Deeside line from Aboyne to Ballater. The route between Kincardine O'Neil and Aboyne remains to be completed in order for the path to run almost the whole of the distance from Aberdeen to Ballater.

Excursion trains were very popular in the early part of the 20th century. This might well be a young Aberdonian dressed in his Sunday best enjoying a holiday in Banchory.

The exterior of the Joint Station of Aberdeen in the early 1920s. The station currently standing was built as Aberdeen Joint Station between 1913–16, replacing an 1867 station which occupied the same site. The original station with the newly-extended railway line from Kittybrewster through the Denburn Valley, enabled the main line from the south and the line from Deeside to connect with the line from the north. The lines from the south had previously terminated at the adjacent Aberdeen Guild Street. Even this had not been Aberdeen's first railway station, that distinction belonging to a previous terminus a short way south at Ferryhill. Today the concourse is no longer and a new integrated train and bus station and retail complex, Union Square, occupies the site.

The foundation stone of the new Joint Railway Station building in Aberdeen was laid on 28th May 1913. Demolition of the station roof of the old Joint Station began in August 1913 and was carried on with minimum disruption to service. A wooden trolley with two cranes on top was used. By July of the following year all the new platforms were in use. Some 190 men worked on the demolition of the old building and construction of the new one. The bulk of the material was freestone from Northumberland but some Kemnay granite was also used.

Lying alongside the crowded railway tracks is Union Terrace Gardens, sometimes known as *the trainie park*, opened in 1879. The area is not a natural amphitheatre but a small river valley with a late-Victorian viaduct constructed at the north end in 1889. The photo dates from 1900 – Central Library and St. Mark's Church can be seen but His Majesty's Theatre is missing – it was not opened until December 1906. Alongside the Gardens a crowded railway layout – two mail vans, (one with pick-up gear) are on the right and on the left two-tone rolling stock. Heaps of ash lie alongside the turntable. The scene is very different today – the railway has been reduced to a single track and all that remains of the turntable is the pit.

The view in 1907 looking across Union Bridge to Union Terrace Gardens with, in the distance, the Central Library, St. Mark's Church, and the newly opened His Majesty's Theatre. Aberdonians often refer to these three buildings as *Education*, *Salvation* and *Damnation*. Next to the theatre on the right is Schoolhill Station which opened in 1893. From 1907 until 1917 one of the suburban evening trains from Culter ran on to this station to allow passengers to attend a performance at the theatre with a conveniently timed return later in the evening.

Ferryhill was the terminus of the Aberdeen Railway from the south and was opened on 16th March 1850. It was from here that the first timetabled train left on Thursday 8th September 1853 bound for Banchory. The station at Ferryhill was always regarded as temporary and it closed on 2nd August 1854, being replaced by Guild Street Station and later the Joint Station which opened in 1867. At Ferryhill the old Caledonian engine shed, dating from 1852, can still be seen. Until 1920 Royal Trains, seldom entered the Joint Station preferring to use Ferryhill Junction for exchanging engines. The Ferryhill Railway Heritage Trust was set up in 2007 to take over the remaining building and turntable with the aim to restore it and transform the site into a working railway heritage site for the north east of Scotland. From Ferryhill the line then travelled west passing Duthie Park, which was gifted to the city by Miss. Elizabeth Crombie Duthie of Ruthrieston. The park was opened by Princess Beatrice, the youngest daughter of Queen Victoria, on 27th September 1883, when a public holiday was declared. After touring the park on a particularly wet and windy day, Princess Beatrice left for Balmoral by train from a specially-constructed platform near the Mound.

On 27th September 1906 King Edward VII and Queen Alexandra came by Royal Train from Ballater to Holburn Street Station which was lavishly decorated for the occasion. Leaving from the station in an open carriage the King and Queen made their way through the decorated streets of Aberdeen to open the extended Marischal College then part of Aberdeen University and from 2011 the headquarters of Aberdeen City Council. Its granite frontage, which encloses the quadrangle, is the second largest granite building in the world, exceeded only by the Escorial Palace near Madrid. Again on 29th September 1929 Holburn Street Station was used by King George V and Queen Mary when they alighted there on their way to the opening of the extension to the Art Gallery and Cowdray Hall. On both occasions the return journey to Ballater was made from the Joint Station. The name Holburn Street is named after the Howburn over which it passes and has nothing to do with the Holburn of London.

Ruthrieston Station was typical of stations built at that time – on one platform a wooden building with a hipped roof and a simple waiting room on the other. The wooden footbridge is in the distance. It was opened in 1856 as an additional stop on the new Deeside Line and was one of the stops of the suburban railway which started operating in 1894 and ceased in 1937. Before reaching Cults there was a station at Pitfodels, opened in 1894 as a stop on the suburban service to Culter. It was downgraded to a halt in 1927 because of insufficient passenger numbers.

Cults Stations in the early 1900s with a non-stop train passing through on its way to Ballater. 'Picturesque Deeside begins at Cults', wrote the *Aberdeen Journal* in 1886, 'nowhere is the Aberdonian craze for building houses, fine houses too – more forcible illustrated'. Thus Cults grew rapidly in the early 20th century thanks to the suburban service which took passengers to town in only 12 minutes. The Aberdeen-bound platform had a booking office, waiting room and staff accommodation. Originally the other platform had no shelter but this was provided in 1884. A wooden footbridge connecting the two platforms was replaced in the 1930s by a metal one. The station buildings remain. *Bradshaw's Railway Handbook* of 1861 suggests that the name Cults comes from the Celtic word *quilques* meaning a corner. Alternatively the name may be derived from the Gaelic *cuillte* meaning recess. South of the station was St. Devenick's Bridge – more commonly known as the *Shakkin' Briggie*. It was built in 1837 at a cost of £1400 from funds provided by Dr. George Morison, minister of Banchory-Devenick Church. His parish extended over both sides of the Dee and the bridge replaced a boat which brought parishioners from the north side of the river to the church on the south. The high floods of 1958 ruined the foundations and the bridge was closed to pedestrians. No funds have since been made available to restore it. A short distance west of the station an additional stop, West Cults, was built when the suburban service opened in 1894.

Bieldside Station was built to meet the need of this residential district as it developed. It was opened on 1st June 1897 and commanded one of the best views in the district which is reflected in the name Bieldside – from the Gaelic *bield* – the sheltered side. The Stationmaster's House is on the left of the platform. To the south was Bieldside Golf Course and in the early days, before motor cars became more common, many golfers used the service from Aberdeen to take them to the golf course which is immediately adjacent to the station. There was competition to the railway from the Aberdeen Suburban Tramways Company which opened a service in June 1904 from Mannofield in Aberdeen out as far as Bieldside.

Murtle was one of the original stations of the line to Banchory but when the suburban service was withdrawn in 1937, it closed along with another six of the intermediate stations. This then left only Cults as a stop between Culter and Aberdeen. The old station is now a private house. The station was used by visitors to the Deeside Hydropathic which was about half a mile to the north and opened in 1899. After the Second World War it was renamed Tor-na-Dee and treated ex-service men and women suffering from pulmonary tuberculosis. Subsequently it was a convalescent hospital. The area is now known as Woodland Grove and provides housing for the over 55s. Murtle gets its name from the Gaelic *mor-choille* – big wood. Murtle House, which is nearby, was built for John Thorburn to the design of the architect Archibald Simpson. The house, one of the finest classical house on Deeside, now forms part of the Rudolf Steiner School.

Milltimber another of the suburban stations, saw increased usage after the building of Maryculter Bridge in 1895, which allowed residents on the south bank to make use of the railway. In 1936 special trains which took passengers from Inverurie and Aberdeen to Milltimber for the Boy Scouts' Rally at Templars' Park on 26th September when Lord Baden-Powell opened the camping ground of the City of Aberdeen. Here we see a *subby*, as they were fondly known, passing another train at the station. The message on the reverse of the postcard written at Milltimber Station on 8th April 1915 recalls that it was on 'the 10th April that the *Titanic* sailed on her fateful voyage (three years earlier) – I will not say more just now'. One can only surmise the reasons for the writer including this curious statement on the card. It may well be a reference to Sir Cosmo Duff-Gordon of Maryculter House, now a hotel, who was one of those rescued from the *Titanic*. Many stories have been told about how he managed to be saved but on returning home he became something of a recluse.

Culter from the Railway Bridge.

The building on the Aberdeen-bound platform at Culter consisted of a booking office, waiting hall and staff accommodation while on the opposite platform there was a simple waiting shelter. A wooden footbridge linked the two platforms. Culter owed its development to industry rather than to tourism. Bartholomew Smith began the manufacture of paper here in 1751. There was a siding leading to the entrance to the mill as early as 1864 and by the turn of the century what might be termed a branch line had been laid. The railway handled a considerable amount of the paper mill output and although the passenger service from Culter ceased in February 1966 there was a stay of execution until 30th December 1966 for trade from the mill.

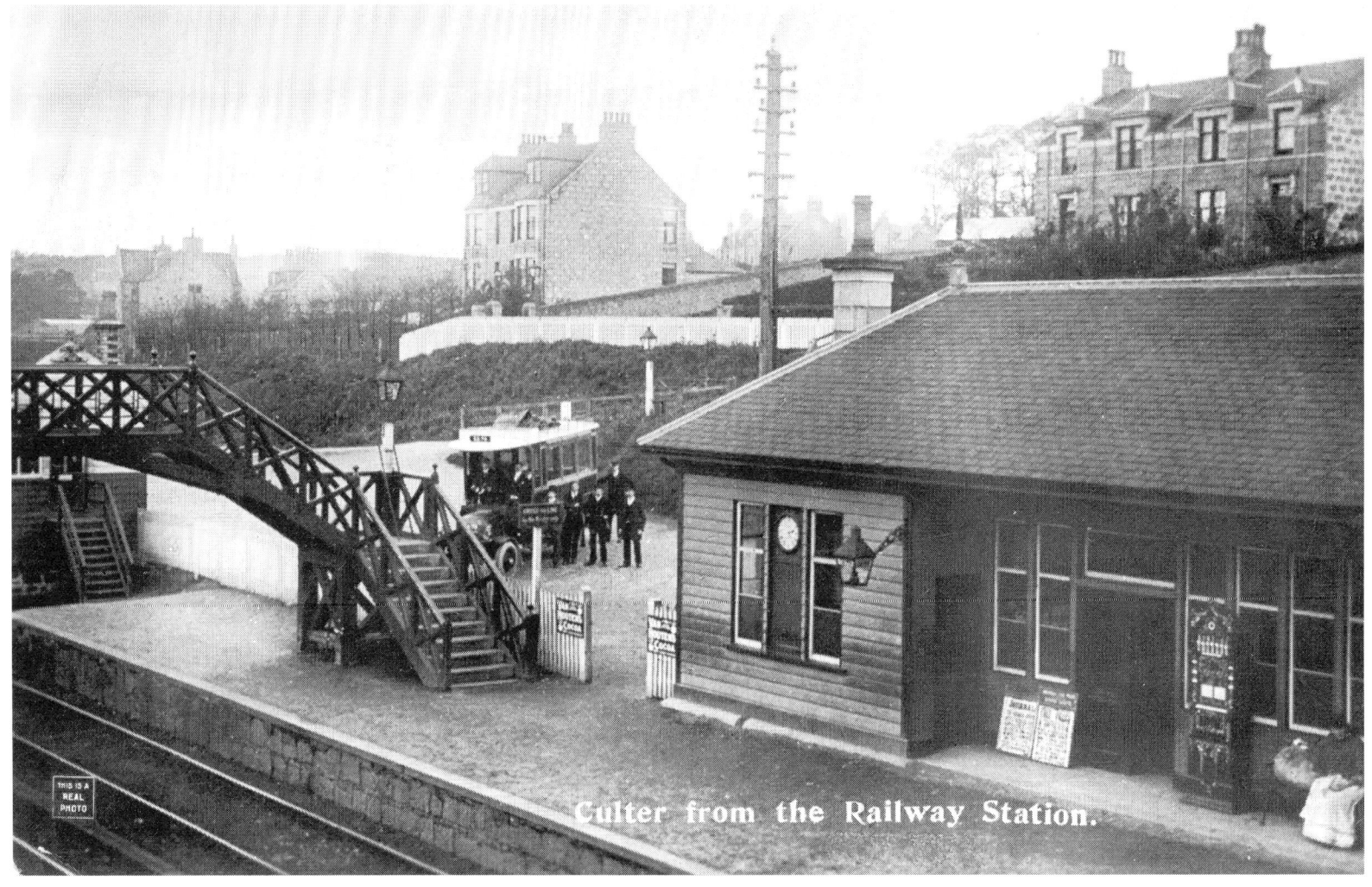

Awaiting the arrival of the train to take some passengers onwards, to Midmar, is a Milnes-Daimler bus, registration number SA74. This service was operated by the Great North of Scotland Railway Company from June 1905 until November 1906 when it was replaced by a direct service from Aberdeen to Midmar. The Milnes-Daimler bus was then transferred to the Ballater-Braemar service. Above the station are the two granite villas of East Brae and West Brae.

The station staff at Culter in February 1914. King William the Lion gave the lands of Culter, on both sides of the Dee, to the monks of the Abbey of St. Mary of Kelso. A century later in 1287–1288, an agreement was made between the Abbot of Kelso and the Knights of Jerusalem regarding the Templar lands on the south side of the Dee. It was this agreement that created the two parishes with separate names, Peterculter and Maryculter. It was possible pre-1937 to reach the railway station from Maryculter. The ferrywoman *Boatie Maggie* – Margaret Irvine – would take you for 1d to the churchyard of St. Peter's Church, now a Heritage Museum.

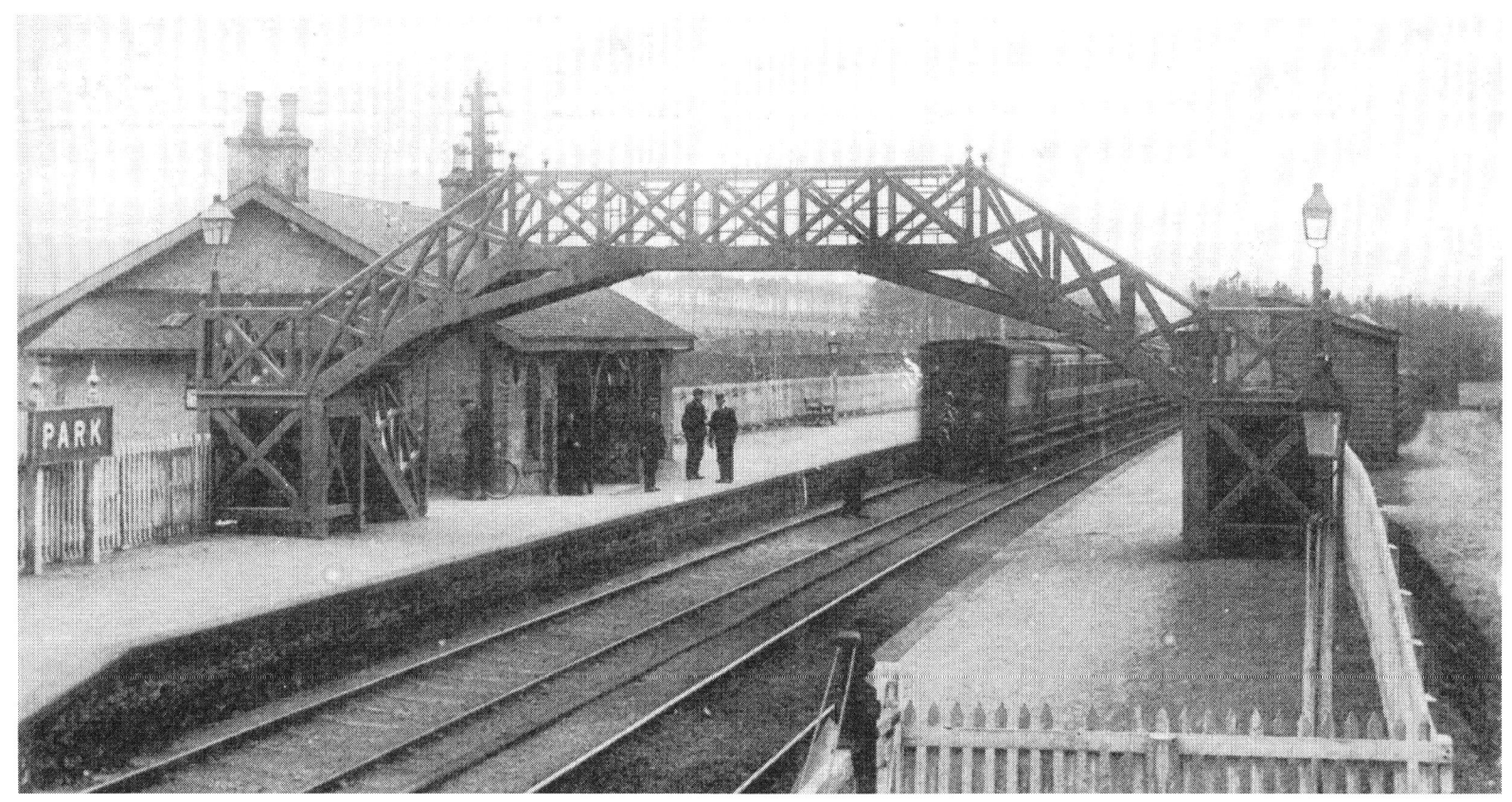

A mile after Drum was the station at Park. Close by is Park House. When Robert the Bruce granted part of the Royal Forest of Drum to William de Irvine in 1323, he reserved certain rights in the Park for himself. His grandson, Robert II granted the whole of the Park to the Irvines in 1389 and it remained in their possession until 1737. In 1839 Alexander John Low became proprietor under rather unusual circumstances. James Kinloch, a native of Kincardineshire who had made his fortune in India, died a bachelor and left a substantial sum of money to the family of his sister, a Mrs. Low, on the understanding that it would be invested in the purchase of land in Scotland and that his heir would assume the name of Kinloch. Hence Alexander Low became a Kinloch. On 5th July 1852, his wife cut the first turf for the building of the railway on land close to the house. A road linking the Deeside Turnpike via the Park Bridge to the parish of Durris on the south bank of the River Dee was laid out by the Deeside Railway Company in order to encourage passengers and freight from that side of the river. A metal plate on the south west girder of the bridge reads 'James Abernethy & Co., Ferryhill Foundry, Aberdeen, 1854'. One half-penny for a foot passenger, one penny for a passenger with a bicycle and threepence for a motor car was charged for the use of the bridge. British Rail continued to collect the tolls right up to the mid-1950s. The bridge was the last toll bridge in use in Aberdeenshire. The station and line remained open to the final closure of the line in 1966.

For another three and a half miles the route followed the turnpike road closely with a stop at Mills of Drum, a station which only remained open from 1853 for 10 years, before reaching Crathes. The railway signalman's house was moved to Crathes Estate and called Kashentroch but was seriously damaged in a fire in 2002 and demolished. The view here of the station at Crathes is looking west and dates from the early 1900s. The name Crathes is derived from the Gaelic *craichidh* meaning boggy ground. Crathes Castle is the traditional home of the Burnett family, lairds of Leys, on land originally given by Robert the Bruce in 1323 to Alexander de Burnard. The castle, a National Trust for Scotland property since 1952, is within easy reach. The old Durris Bridge was built in 1862 by Alexander Mactier, then proprietor of Durris, to provide access from Durris to Crathes Station. Although Mactier bore the whole cost of the bridge he made a charge for its use in order, as he claimed, 'that those of his tenants who crossed at the Park Bridge would not be disadvantaged'. This charge, however, soon fell into abeyance.

Originally this was a private halt for the Laird of Crathes until the station was built in 1863. A condition of the feu charter granted to the railway company for the building of the public station was that all trains should stop at Crathes. This led to a dispute between Sir Robert Burnett of Leys and the railway company. Messenger trains ran on the line from 1865 to 1937 to carry despatches to the Queen and later Kings at Balmoral. By 1878 these services were being included in the timetables and in 1883 this led to a lawsuit because these trains and also an excursion train to Banchory were not stopping at Crathes. The railway company initially won the case but this was partially reversed in 1885 following an appeal to the House of Lords. It was ruled that the Messenger train had to make a stop at Crathes but the excursion was allowed to pass as it was not available to passengers with ordinary tickets. In 1914 Sir Thomas Burnett of Leys waived his rights and as a result some of the fast regular trains no longer had to stop. It is believed that one of the early Messenger trains had an engine painted in Royal Stewart tartan and that the coaches displayed the Queen's Coat of Arms. In 1969 after the line had closed three years earlier, Malcolm Appleby the renowned engraver and silversmith bought the old station and made it his home and workshop for the next 27 years.

In 1996 the Royal Deeside Railway Preservation Society was formed with the aim of restoring a section of the line from Milton of Crathes to Banchory, a total distance of just over two miles. In 2012 the Victorian station building, which originally stood at Oldmeldrum, was moved to Milton and reconstructed. It now houses a shop, ticket office and waiting room. At present, one mile of track has been restored and the Society operates diesel engines and two steam locomotives – *Bon Accord*, built for the Aberdeen Corporation Gasworks in 1897, and *Salmon* shown here. *Salmon*, built in 1942, is named after HMS *Salmon*, a British submarine which in December 1939 sighted the German liner SS *Bremen*. The commander of the *Salmon* decided not to torpedo the liner because he believed she was not a legal target. His decision not to fire on *Bremen* possibly delayed the start of unrestricted submarine warfare in the war. Alongside the engine is the Battery Railcar introduced in 1958 on the Deeside Line. This train was powered by batteries re-charged at Aberdeen and Ballater. In 1962 problems were being experienced with the railcar, and it was withdrawn. In 1984 it was restored to working order and used for some time on the privately-owned East Lancashire Railway, north of Manchester. Although the Society gained ownership of the unit in 2001, it took another five years before it returned to the track. It is hoped that one day the railcar, known locally as the *Sputnik*, will be able under its own power to operate on this section of the old Deeside line.

A tranquil scene on the track at a bend of the Dee near Banchory. A man is seen fishing for salmon off the north bank with two ladies possibly watching from the edge of the track. On the south two small islands formed subsequent to the great flood in the year 1769. The largest one is low and flat and extends to almost nine acres, sometimes becoming nearly submerged by high floods; the smaller island is more elevated and consists mostly of sand and is covered by trees. In the distance Scolty with its tower on the summit erected in 1842 in memory of General William Burnett of Banchory Lodge, brother of Sir Robert Burnett of Leys, 7th Baronet of Crathes.

Prior to the reconstruction of the station at Banchory in 1902, preparatory work was undertaken by building a retaining wall with a right of way path alongside the Dee, known as the 'Platties'. The name platties comes from the Scot's word *plat* meaning a flat spot. Stones were taken in by railway wagons and tipped down the embankment before being craned on to bogies which conveyed them along a temporary track behind the wall where they were lifted into place by a crane.

Banchory Station was reconstructed in 1902 with wider platforms, extended facilities and a covered footbridge. This was obviously necessary since James Coutts, writing in *A Dictionary of Deeside* in 1899 called it a 'station which is neither well built nor well situated, being placed at the eastern outskirts close to the churchyard, as if designed for nearness to the dead rather than the living'. St. Ternan's 7th century settlement was centred on the site of the churchyard which became the focus of the medieval Parish of Banchory-Ternan. The name Banchory corresponds to the Welsh and Cornish Bangors and shares the same original meaning of a Christian settlement within a wattled/plaited enclosure. Within the churchyard is the watchtower, built in 1829, used to guard against body snatchers. A housing estate now fills the space occupied by the station which was demolished in 1970. The engine sheds to the east remain the sole surviving building of the Deeside Railway Company. Since 1994, they have been used by Roy Cowie, a landscape services company, who has two Royal Warrants. The old engine sheds now proudly display the coat of arms of HM The Queen and the badge of Prince Charles, Duke of Rothesay, as Prince of Wales. Near the engine sheds, there was a turntable and a second water tower.

Banchory soon developed into a popular place for visitors and from the opening of the line in 1853 special excursion trains were popular. In July 1854 it was reported that '56 carriages took 1,700, along the beautiful route of the Deeside line – for the most part to Banchory'. In Alex McConnachie's *Deeside* published in 1900, the author refers to it as 'a summer resort for Aberdonians and tourists which takes precedence, for numbers, over all others, while on holidays excursionists visit it literally in thousands. The Hill of Fare protects Banchory from the cold winds of the north and its southern exposure also contributes to its advantages as a health and holiday resort. Unquestionably nature has done a great deal for Banchory; the marvel is that the century had begun [that is, the 19th century] before the nucleus of a town had been founded in such a delightful situation'.

The view at Banchory looking north soon after the new station was completed in 1902. Goods traffic was important to the station and in the foreground coal is being unloaded while in the distance, top right is the Station Hotel (until 1878 the old Loanhead School). In front was the Free Church mentioned in the original act of 1852 as the terminating point of the first section of the Deeside Railway. The Free Church moved to the centre of Banchory in 1880. In 1854 the firm of Messrs. A & G Paterson Ltd built a mill about half a mile east of Banchory Station alongside the new railway line at Silverbank, then known as Silverstripe (Stripe is the burn which flows into the Dee near this point). Timber for many years was floated down the river but with the coming of the railway to Banchory in 1853 and the later extensions to Aboyne and Ballater, the work of the wood floaters was greatly reduced. On the river bank below the sawmills one can still see the old stones with iron rings for tying up the timber rafts. The sawmill continues to trade under the name James Cordiner & Son Ltd.

In 1901 Banchory was very much a rural village with a population given in the census of about 1,500. The 20th century saw the development of the town to the west of the station and with a population now of almost 9,000, it remains attractive with magnificent scenery all around. In 1961 a halt was built at the corner of Bridge Street and Dee Street in an attempt to gain more traffic to the town centre but it was too late to make any real impact before the line closed in 1966. This picture, from the early 1950s, shows the railway embankment with Banchory in the background. The three railway bridges over Dee Street, Kinneskie Road leading to the golf course, and at the west end of the High Street, have long since gone.

The motto of Banchory, *Bydand* meaning Steadfast, is that of the Gordon Highlanders. The village has close associations with the Regiment and it was from the station in Banchory that on 16th April 1915, 130 men of the 7th Gordon Highlanders left to join their Battalion at Bedford and be kitted out for what was to lie ahead. Seeing them off is a Gordons' Pipe Band dressed in khaki aprons over their kilts. The Battalion crossed to France and as part of the 51st Highland Division took part courageously in most of the battles of the Great War. On the North Deeside Road to the left of the old railway line as you leave Banchory, these battles are remembered on a memorial to honour the men of the 7th (Deeside) Battalion Gordon Highlanders who gave their lives.

This Royal Train is passing through the outskirts of Banchory on its way to Ballater, with Scolty Hill in the background, probably in the 1920s in the early days of LNER. The first Royal Train left Banchory on 11th October 1853 with Queen Victoria's mother, the Duchess of Kent. During her several journeys to and from Abergeldie Castle and later Balmoral, the Duchess frequently rested at the Burnett Arms and her coat-of-arms is above the entrance to the hotel. It was reported in *The Scotsman* of Wednesday 20th September 1854 that Queen Victoria on her annual journey to Balmoral went with Prince Albert and the Royal children to the 'refreshment rooms where luncheon was served in very elegant style by Mr. Grant of the Burnett Arms Inn'. HM The Queen left on the last Royal Train from Ballater on 15th October 1965. It is well documented that Dwight D Eisenhower, first as General and later as President, visited the Royal Family at Balmoral. In October 1946, HM King George VI hosted General Eisenhower and his wife and again in August 1959, as President Eisenhower, he spent the night at Balmoral as a guest of HM Queen Elizabeth. On both of these occasions Eisenhower travelled to and from Balmoral by car from Dyce Airport in Aberdeen. What is not well known is that General Eisenhower, Supreme Commander of the Allied Expeditionary Force, paid an earlier visit to Deeside. On mid-April 1944 he spent a few days in Banchory, travelling there in the private train which he used during the Second World War. The General enjoyed a mini holiday while preparing for D-Day in June that year. He also went fly fishing for salmon at Cairnton, about two miles west of Banchory, on the River Dee.

The station at Glassel was opened in December 1859 when the Deeside Railway was extended to Aboyne. Just why a station was built there is a mystery but it must be remembered that although there were few houses in the immediate vicinity the railway served a wider community who were dependent on it for their transport. The old station and the adjoining property, which was occupied by the stationmaster, are now private houses.

Before reaching Torphins there was, until 1887, a private halt at Craigmyle House used by the residents and visitors. Torphins may have got its name from Thorfin, Jarl of Orkney and a cousin of King Duncan and Macbeth. Having defeated King Duncan in battle somewhere on the Morayshire coast, Thorfin pursued the remnants of the King's army south and at a place which now bears his name he rested before returning home to Orkney. The railway to Lumphanan followed an earlier plan later abandoned, to build a line from Banchory to Alford via Cushnie. Col. Thomas Innes of Learney recognised the potential of the coming of the railway to Torphins in 1859 and welcomed its construction over his land. At that time Torphins consisted of a few thatched cottages and an old inn but its development following the arrival of the railway was dramatic. With the closure of the line the old station site is now occupied by housing and the road layout has reverted to what it once was.

Railway Viaduct, Torphins

Leaving Torphins the line passed through a cutting before moving out over a five span viaduct at Balnacraig, high over the Beltie Burn. The line then continued into a steep rocky cutting at Tillychin, known as Satan's Den. Although the Deeside Line was closed in 1966, it was not until 1989 that the viaduct was demolished. It had been expected that it would take a week to complete the job but when the first arch across the Tornaveen road was taken down the others fell like a set of dominoes. Within half-an-hour the viaduct had fallen and the famous landmark was no more.

Lumphanan is a village of ancient origin and derives its name from the Welsh *llan* a church or enclosure and Finan, the Welsh missionary and disciple of St. Mungo who brought Christianity to these parts in the 7th century. Lumphanan owes much to the building of the Deeside Railway which was opened from Banchory to Aboyne on 2nd December 1859. The station was a busy place and in its day had a stationmaster, a signalman and a porter. With the arrival of the railway the old Kirkton of Lumphanan was not only left stranded half-a-mile west of the railway station but it was separated from the old St. Finan's Kirk by the intervening railway line. Thus the development of a new village started at the expense of this now rural area. On the left beyond the railway can be seen the Lumphanan Hotel, now known as the Macbeth Arms, and next door with the four distinctive arches a licensed grocer at one time owned by Albert F Law. The building next with the imposing portico was the former Town & County Bank – today Lumphanan is without a bank. The association of Macbeth with Lumphanan is that it was on the slopes of Perkhill, north of the station, that in 1057 he met his death in a hand-to-hand struggle with Macduff.

On the ground adjacent to the station at Lumphanan, and served by the branch line in the foreground, were the agricultural sheds and mart (established in 1911), the lime company and oil storage tanks. All of this added greatly to the use of the station for the forwarding of goods. Between 1864 and 1938 this decreased dramatically from 2,639 tons to 267 tons. Livestock too was carried, but by 1938 this had ceased altogether and goods trains stopped using the station in June 1964. The whole of the old railway site is now occupied by housing. On leaving Lumphanan the railway headed south west, passing Dess, a place with no village and only a few scattered farms. The station building, however, does survive and is now a private house. Dess was the nearest station to Kincardine O' Neil which was bypassed by the railway.

When conditions were right at Aboyne, the Great North of Scotland Railway Company used to lay on special trains from Aberdeen and used a temporary platform which between 1888 and 1930 was used in the summer for excursions and in the winter for bonspiels. The scene is typical of the day – the men well dressed for the occasion. The curler throwing his stone is using the *crampit* (footboard) to save him falling flat on his face. The brooms used by the players to brush the ice are somewhat different from those used today and are very much the typical witch's broom. Curling, some would claim, originated in Scotland, and the name is derived from the ability to make the stone curl by *birling* (turning) the handle of the stone as the player releases the stone. Because of the distinctive sound of the stone as it makes its way along the ice, curling is often referred to as the 'roaring game'.

The Deeside Extension Railway to Aboyne was opened in December 1859 and on 8th August 1860 Queen Victoria travelled north from Edinburgh and for the first time travelled on to Aboyne. The *Aberdeen Journal* reported that the speed so far as Banchory was fast but on coming to the new Deeside Extension line, upon which Her Majesty had not previously travelled, the rate of movement was slackened, and a series of views of scenery probably not equalled on any other railway were very satisfactorily obtained. The station buildings at that time were different from the Victorian rebuilt station of the 1890s as shown on the right. Happily this building still remains with a new housing development to the rear. The derivation of the name Aboyne has always been a matter of conjecture but in all probability it relates to a personal name Obeyn.

The railway track on the approach to Aboyne from the east in the late 19th century, as well as the signal box, station buildings and extensive goods yard to the right of the station. Camping coaches, offering accommodation for 4 - 6 people, were introduced on the line in 1935 and were sited at Murtle, Crathes, Banchory and Cambus O' May and later at Torphins, Aboyne and Ballater. After the war they became less popular and the last one was located at Aboyne until 1960.

Special trains were very much a feature of the Deeside Line for events like the Aboyne Games and Sunday School picnics. Shown here are members of the Aberdeen Battalion of the Boys' Brigade arriving at Aboyne on their way to their annual summer camp, circa 1909, possibly at Craigendinnie south of the river which was used by the Battalion for many years.

The line left Aboyne through the only tunnel on the route and for the next four-and-a-half miles followed the line of the road to Dinnet. Like so many of the stations, Dinnet owes its position to the closeness of an estate, this time the Dinnet Estate. Dinnet House can be seen top right on the north bank of the River Dee. The name of the village is from the Gaelic *dianaid* meaning rapid and refers to the river. The bridge shown dates from 1862 and leads to the South Deeside Road. It was replaced by a new one in 1935. Sir Malcolm Barclay-Harvey of Dinnet served as Governor of South Australia from 1939 - 44. An avid railway enthusiast he wrote *A History of the Great North of Scotland Railway*, published in 1940. The old station now serves as the Estate Office. In 1867 Alfred Nobel discovered that the highly volatile nitroglycerine liquid could be soaked up by diatomite sometimes known as kieselguhr. This substance could then be rolled into sticks and so dynamite was invented. Diatomite was found at Black Moss north of Dinnet, and a small industry sprung up which ran successfully from 1867 to 1910. In a dry state, the diatomite was taken to Dinnet and sent on by train to Ardeer, on the Ayrshire coast, to be processed. The story is told of a stationmaster during the reign of Queen Victoria who held very strict views on the Sabbath and disapproved strongly about any trains travelling on the line on a Sunday. He had, however, to turn a blind eye to the Messenger trains that carried the Queen's mails.

Cambus O' May Station was perched on a narrow shelf overlooking the river. In the early 1900s the directors of the Great North of Scotland Railway held occasional board meetings in a coach shunted into the siding adjoining the main line. The station was at times used for a special delivery service of explosives used for blasting in the nearby pink granite quarry. The old station is now used as a holiday home. The name Cambus O' May literally means bend in the plain which well describes the place. Prior to 1905 a ferry had to be used to cross the river but in that year a suspension bridge, partly funded by the railway company, provided access to the station for passengers from the south side of the river. This is the bridge which can be seen in the distance. With the closure of the line the bridge fell into disrepair and in 1988 it was replaced by a new bridge which did not span the old railway. In the storms of December 2015, the bridge was badly damaged and awaits repair. Leaving Cambus O' May, the line passes the front of Old Ferry Inn, now known as Cutaway Cottage. When the railway was built the north-east corner of the cottage gable was demolished to allow trains to pass. Before reaching Ballater, the old line passed Tullich Kirkyard with its Pictish stones.

Ballater is a comparatively modern village dating from around 1798, the name coming from the Gaelic *baille challater*, town of the wooded stream. It owes its origin to the popularity of the Pannanich Wells, which were believed to have great curative properties, and the need to develop accommodation for the many visitors who came to take the waters. At first the station was a simple booking office on a single platform but in 1886 the station was rebuilt. The architectural guide for Deeside described it thus – 'built in clapboard with deep eaves forming a canopy with decorative bargeboards, also featuring on slender entrance front porte-cochere'. Having fallen into disuse after the closure of the station in 1966 it was refurbished and used as an area office by the local District Council. In 2002, after extensive refurbishment the station buildings were re-opened as a visitor centre including the local tourist office. In May 2015 a disastrous fire destroyed most of the building. Plans have been prepared to restore the station with the hope that it may be completed by the end of 2017. Opposite the station are solid granite buildings given to the people of Ballater by Alexander Gordon, a wealthy brewer of London, and native of Glenmuick. The central portion is known as the Gordon Institute. On the right are the Victoria Halls and on the left is the Albert Memorial Hall.

Queen Victoria leaving Ballater Station for Balmoral in September 1897 on the occasion of her Diamond Jubilee. Her final visit to her *dear paradise in the Highlands* was in 1900 when she was to stay at the Castle until Tuesday 6th November. In the Royal waiting room which had been added in 1886 there was, prior to its destruction in the fire in May 2015, a static display of the occasion. The Queen was dressed in her habitual black and insisted that she wanted to leave privately with no fuss and with no one on the platform. She left that afternoon for Windsor and died just over two months later on 22nd January 1901. During her reign Queen Victoria visited Balmoral every year, using from 1853 Banchory and from 1860 Aboyne as the terminus. After the death of Prince Albert in 1861 she often travelled north twice a year – spring and autumn-using the station at Ballater for the first time in 1867. Royalty from other countries also alighted at Ballater on their way to Balmoral including The Shah of Persia in 1889 and the Czar and Czarina of Russia in 1896.

On Tuesday 9th August 1910 only a few months after accession, King George V and Queen Mary made their first visit to Balmoral. The King is seen here at Ballater Station with two of his sons the sixteen-year-old Prince Edward, later to be King Edward VIII, and his brother the fourteen-year-old Prince Albert, later King George VI. Before leaving for Balmoral the King inspected the Guard of Honour lined up in the square and then the royal party joined the carriages, seen in the background, which took them to Balmoral.

A typical wintry scene at Ballater with all the railway staff out clearing the track so that trains could run as normal. Occasionally, however, the trains failed to run. This was the case in January 1960 during a period of an extremely large snowfall which blocked the route for almost a week. Railcars could make no impression and it was left to a steam train to clear the route. This had an effect on school pupils travelling from Ballater to Banchory Academy. In 1925 the Education Authorities of Kincardineshire and Aberdeenshire agreed to raise the status of the school at Banchory to full six-year secondary level catering for all senior pupils from Culter to Braemar. Pupils used the train daily from as far away as Ballater, some even having to take the bus from Braemar to join up with the train. In the snowstorm of 1960 some senior pupils were stranded at Torphins on their way home and had to spend a couple of days there before reaching home safely.

Ballater Station had a long curving platform, large enough to accommodate the Royal Train. In 1919 the train carrying King George V and the family consisted of twelve coaches. The platform looked out to an engine shed, turntable and water tower and an extensive goods yard. The view in the early 1910s is from west of the station taken on the bridge built over the proposed line to Braemar. Track was laid beyond the bridge for a short distance ending at buffers, but this is no longer. To join what is left, turn right on leaving the old station and follow the Braemar Road for about 100 yards; turn left along Invercauld Road then right along Drumdarroch Road to the path called Old Line Road which provides a scenic walk along what is left of the track bed as far as Bridge of Gairn.

By 1868 the ground from Ballater to Bridge of Gairn was being prepared for the goods railway intended to carry timber from Ballochbuie Forest, then owned by Col. James Farquharson of Invercauld. A new bridge over the River Gairn had been built for the railway, when without much warning construction on the line was halted. That year the forest was leased for ten years by Queen Victoria and bought outright by her in 1878 to prevent it being bought for the felling of its timber. It is sometimes claimed that saving the forest marked the first woodland conservation project in Scotland. To mark this significant event, the Queen had a cairn erected on the Balmoral Estate. There was no longer the need for the railway to collect the timber and so the proposed railway route from Ballater to Bridge of Gairn never was required. Instead a bus served the route from Ballater to Braemar and the picture shows it at Bridge of Gairn with a full load of passengers complete with the luggage on the roof.